~ POSTCARDS FROM TH

NEWCASTLE-UNDER-LYME
& District

Dennis and Barbara Morris, Tony & Joy Priestley, Roger Simmons and Edward Watkin

Copyright © Dennis and Barbara Morris, Tony & Joy Priestley, Roger Simmons and Edward Watkin, 1998

All Rights Reserved. No part of this publication may be reproduced, stored in a retrieval system, or transmitted in any form or by any means – electronic, mechanical, photocopying, recording, or otherwise – without prior written permission from the publisher.

First published in 1987 as "The Borough of Newcastle-under-Lyme - a portrait in old picture postcards" by Brampton Publications

This fully revised edition is published by Sigma Leisure – an imprint of
Sigma Press, 1 South Oak Lane, Wilmslow, Cheshire SK9 6AR, England.

British Library Cataloguing in Publication Data
A CIP record for this book is available from the British Library.

ISBN: 1-85058-665-9

Typesetting and Design by: Sigma Press, Wilmslow, Cheshire.

Cover photograph: opening day of the tram service to Wolstanton

Printed by: MFP Design and Print

Acknowledgments

Dennis and Barbara Morris, Tony and Joy Priestley, Roger Simmons, Edward Watkin, Miss L.M. Warham and Mr Donald H. Watkin for the loan of their postcards; Dennis Morris, Tony and Joy Priestley, Roger Simmons and Edward Watkin for the original text; Tony Priestley for reviewing the text; Mr G. Barrington for his assistance with some of the research on Silverdale.

Original editorial by Steve Benz. Thanks also, the Sigma Press team for their meticulous editing and design skills which have permitted this book to be reissued in its revised form.

PREFACE

The Borough of Newcastle-under-Lyme, as it exists today, comprises an area steeped in history. With the aim of renewing and further enhancing an interest in the local history, this book, depicting scenes of the area mostly between 1904 and 1935, has been reprinted.

As with most towns in Britain, vast areas of Newcastle have changed dramatically over the past ninety years. Many buildings, landmarks and whole areas have disappeared as a result of redevelopment, slum clearance, new roads, pit closures and the general shift of industry.

During the original compilation of this book, it was very sad to see that so many of the beautiful buildings in the area such as the Municipal Hall, the Tudor-style buildings in High Street and the two Henry White's stores, had been demolished in the name of 'progress': buildings that were, for many Newcastle people, a permanent part of their lives.

Originally published in 1987 as *The Borough of Newcastle-under-Lyme*, this revised edition uses most of the same postcards although a few of the unclear postcards have either been rephotographed, using more modern technology, or replaced by scenes of the same locality. All the texts have been newly researched and many rewritten, as they were frequently erroneous in view of the changes that have taken place around and in Newcastle-under-Lyme in the intervening years.

We hope this book brings back many happy memories of the Borough of Newcastle-under-Lyme as it was years ago. We would like to thank those residents who have so kindly and willingly given assistance in compiling the texts with their personal memories, details of which are unavailable from reference books or available documentation.

Tony Priestley & Dennis Morris

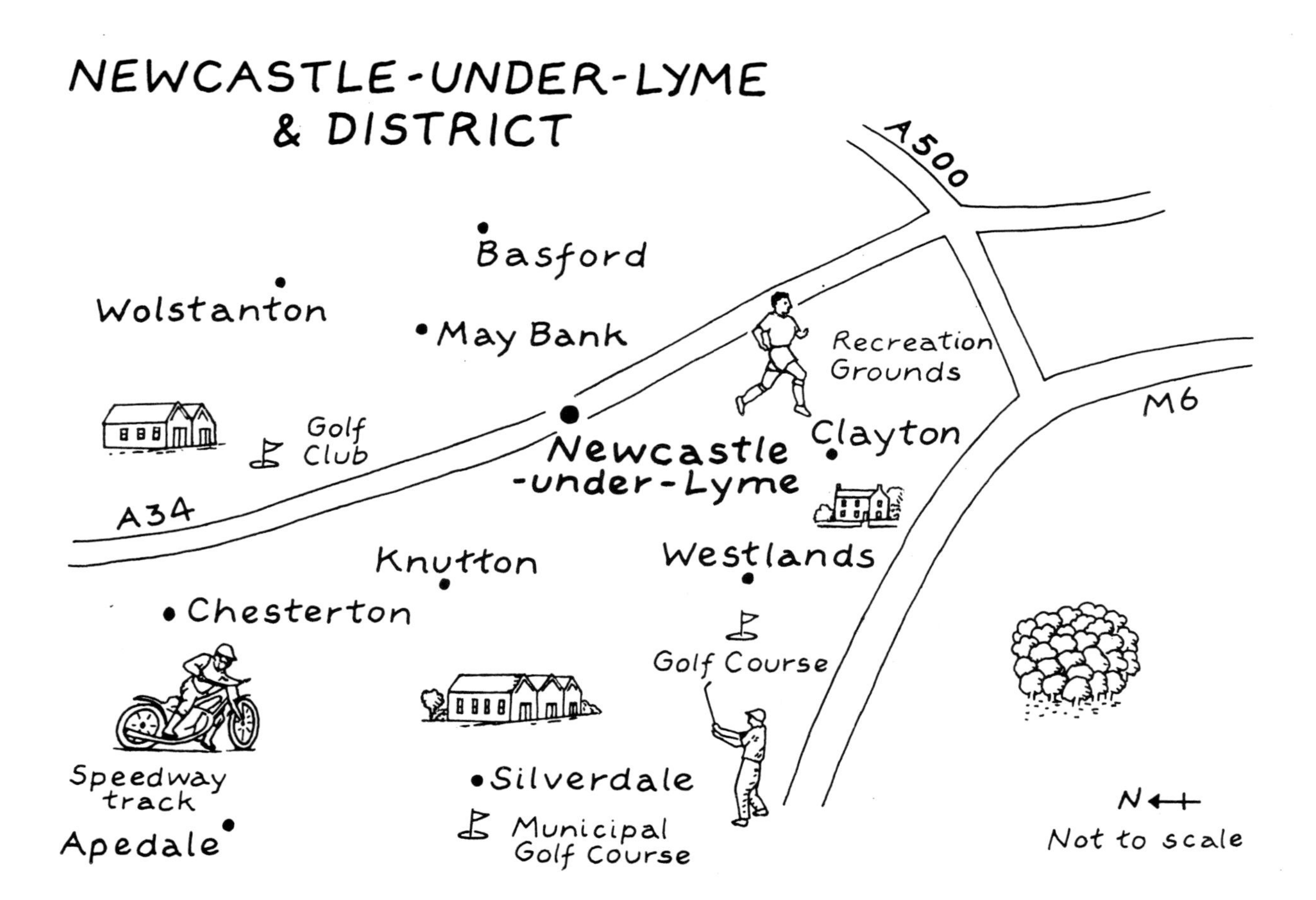
NEWCASTLE-UNDER-LYME
& DISTRICT
A500
Basford
Wolstanton
May Bank
Recreation
Grounds
M6
Golf
Club
Newcastle
-under-Lyme
Clayton
A34
Knutton
Westlands
Chesterton
Golf Course
Speedway
track
Silverdale
Apedale
Municipal
Golf Course
N
Not to scale

CONTENTS

THE COAT OF ARMS OF NEWCASTLE–UNDER–LYME

The permission for the adoption of the Coat of Arms was granted by Queen Elizabeth the First on 18th May, 1519.

It was based on the seal granted by Henry the Third in 1235 to the burgesses of Newcastle, who had formed a merchant guild.

The centre coat of arms showing the three leopards of England represent Henry the Third. The arms to the right, three golden garbs on a blue background represent the arms of the Earl of Chester, Randle de Blundeville, who was granted the manor of Newcastle from King John. The arms to the left, a lion rampant, represent the royal arms of Cornwall. Richard, Earl of Cornwall and brother to King Henry the Third had a connection with Newcastle in 1235. Two men-at-arms, one holding a horn and the other an axe are on the ramparts of the castle, built in c. 1150. ('New Castle' named to avoid confusion with an older medieval castle at Chesterton, was situated at a strategic junction of the London to Carlisle and Chester roads, close to St. Giles' Church).

The latin motto translated means 'The Common Seal of the burgesses of New Castle'.

THE GLOBE CAFÉ, NEWCASTLE

This nostalgic postcard printed by W. Parton, Hassell Street, Newcastle will bring back many happy memories for the older generation of the district. Illustrated is the 'Globe Café', 55 High Street, Newcastle, now renamed as 'Bar Indigo', a 'Continental Café Bar'.

WOLSTANTON CORONATION PROCESSION, 1911
This rare postcard shows part of the Wolstanton Procession celebrating the Coronation of George V as it passes along Dimsdale Parade heading for Wolstanton Marsh. Note how the people in the photograph splendidly display the fashion of the time. The property remains unaltered today. Between the buildings is Simpson Street, with one extra building being added to the property at each side.

CLAYTON ROAD, NEWCASTLE

CLAYTON ROAD, c. 1930
Clayton Road has been widened since this photograph was taken by W. Parton, a well known Newcastle photographer.
The trees in the foreground have gone and the houses on the right-hand side have lost much of their front gardens. The trees in the background still protect Newcastle cemetery.

NEW ROAD, c. 1928

A cutting was made through the red sandstone to build the new road from the town to Westlands in the late 1920's. This road was soon to be named Priory Road and today the cutting is overgrown with large trees shading the road.

RED LION SQUARE, c. 1925

The Pavilion Cinema was built on the site of a flour mill and auction rooms, and opened in 1922. In 1931, the owner, Mr Robert Beresford, also opened the Regal Cinema next door. Little of this scene has altered, although the cinemas have been demolished to be replaced by Lloyds Bank.

OPENING DAY OF THE TRAM SERVICE TO WOLSTANTON, c. 1905
Here, local dignitaries are posing for this photograph of the second tramcar, run by the 'Potteries Electric Traction Company' to go to Wolstanton. Whose boy was privileged enough to be put in front by the driver? The P.E.T. was incorporated in 1898 using electrically operated tramcars, changing its name to the 'Potteries Motor Traction Company' in 1933. The last tram, superseded by buses, ran in 1923.

KNUTTON SCHOOL, NEWCASTLE, STAFF, 1930s

This church school was constructed in 1874 to serve the community of Knutton after the introduction of free schooling. This photograph of the well-built premises shows the 'Old School House' prominent to the left. At the other side, more modern buildings not on the photograph have enabled the school to be considerably enlarged.

THISTLEBERRY CASTLE, c. 1905

This building stood in the grounds of Thistleberry House, which was at the junction of Keele Road and Thistleberry Avenue. It was built between 1785 and 1847 by Samuel Mayer. The 'castle' was pulled down about 1919 and its bricks were used to fill in the moat. In 1942, a large bomb fell on the site, so that no traces of the building or moat now remain.

THE CLOUGHS, c. 1905
This large house stood at the junction of Gallowstree Lane with Keele Road.
This is another card from the 'Royal' Pictorial Post Card Budget (see page 15).

WHITMORE ROAD, c. 1906
If published today this postcard would be entitled Seabridge Road, Newcastle, viewed from Higherland. Before Priory Road was constructed, this would have been the only direct road from Whitmore into Newcastle. The cottages on either side in the foreground have now disappeared, but the terrace of houses in Seabridge Road remain. The beautiful gas lamp with its stone plinth was obviously an ideal meeting place to discuss the latest news or scandal. Note the advertisement for Reckitt's Blue on the gable wall of the right-hand cottage; memories of "old tyme" washdays.

ST. GILES CHURCH, NEWCASTLE

The original Church was built in 1721. In 1872, the Church was demolished with the exception of the Church tower. The new Church was designed by Sir Gilbert Scott and built on to the Church tower between 1873 and 1876. The pulpit, beautifully carved in oak to the Gothic design by Mr. Thompson of Peterborough, was presented to the Church by Mr. Edward Turner in memory of his father and mother. Mr. John Gallimore presented the communion table, again in oak and supported on twelve pillars, another example of splendid workmanship. The consecration of the Church took place on Ascension Day, 25th May, 1876 at 3 p.m. by the Lord Bishop of Lichfield. At the evening service, Rev. Sir L. T. Stamer, Bart., Rector of Stoke-on-Trent preached the sermon. Collections for the day amounted to £175-18-3d.

RED LION SQUARE, c. 1920

The overall appearance of the buildings shown have changed very little over the years, apart from some renovations and the removal in 1926 of the stone structure in the centre of the picture. This building was at one time the office of the Weights and Measures Inspector. On the left, some beautiful old cars are waiting in the taxi rank and the buildings on the right are : C. J. Wain, Chemist and Druggist, who are still trading today; and the 'Sentinel' branch office, which occupied the same premises as Godwin the Printers and who also still trade today off Red Lion Square. The 'Sentinel' offices advertise 'a net sale of nearly 70,000 per day' and 'Quick and certain results assured', with reference to advertising with the paper.

RED LION SQUARE, c. 1906

This view shows a great deal of activity in the Square.
An electric tram is turning into the square and advertises 'Beresford's motor cycles' and 'Tea' on the front and side sign boards respectively. The two open carriages give evidence to the fact that horse transport was still very much to the fore at this time.
On the right, the tall red brick building was the Globe Hotel. The 'Globe' and the remaining adjacent buildings were demolished in the mid 1960's. A new block of shops were built in their place, with Bookland at 19, High Street being the first shop to open on 14th December, 1967.

CLEMSON'S, RED LION SQUARE, c. 1905
Clemson and Son were known as 'The Popular Cash Drapers'. This postcard is taken from a booklet sold by them. It was described as The 'Royal' Pictorial Post Card Budget and contained twelve views of places of interest in Newcastle-under-Lyme. The booklet price was one penny and the postcards had a perforated end so that they could be detached at will.

OLD TOWN HALL AND MARKET PLACE, c. 1904
This view shows the buildings, which occupied the site now known as Lancaster Buildings, with the Guildhall at the rear. The premises in the left foreground were the Newcastle Gas Offices and the shop adjoining was Hamrouges Tobacconists, with 'Fry's Chocolate' being advertised on one of the windows. The next shop bears the name Scott and on the far corner was the Potteries Motor Traction Company Office, which still occupies this same site in the new building today.

MARKET CROSS, c. 1935

A very clear picture of the Market Cross, which was restored and erected in this position in 1820, with further restoration having taken place in recent years.
The decorative lights shown in this picture, replaced the original wrought iron top at a later date.
The Guildhall has changed very little even today, but the shops of Mandley and Unett, Printers and Stationers and Marsden Bros., Merchant Tailors, Outfitters and Hatters, alas, are no longer with us.
However, the Savoy cinema remains and Oxens the Chemists have re-located their shop in another part of High Street. Note the two old Potteries buses in the background.

MAYOR CHOOSING, 1908

The Mayor choosing took place every Charter day until c. 1932, with the Mayor, Civic dignitaries and members of the Council assembled around the Market Cross. There is so much of interest in this picture, it is difficult to know what to highlight. The Mace Bearers can be seen towards the front of the group, as can the local constabulary, note also the dress of the children. To the rear of the cross, is the double-fronted shop of Mellard and Sons, Ironmongers and to the right, Johnson Brothers, Dyers and Cleaners.

HIGH STREET

A typical scene in High Street on market day in the early 1930's, and obviously before the days of pedestrianisation, by passes or double yellow lines.
The cars on view would be the envy of any collector today and the one in the foreground is "double parked".
Note the sign on the Guild Hall for the Castle Hotel and Garage, which is AA and RAC listed.
The Castle Hotel with its boxed bays can be seen on the right of the picture.

HIGH STREET, c. 1904
"All the fun of the fair" in High Street, Newcastle.
This postcard shows a view looking down High Street from near to its junction with Friar Street.
Where did the photographer position the camera? The Guildhall is a possibility, but would such a good picture have resulted from that distance in the early days of photography?
A boxing booth, swing boats, roundabouts and numerous side shows are crammed into High Street.
The event appeared to be well patronised with everyone wearing their Sunday best.

HIGH STREET

Looking at this view of High Street before the advent of the trams, one can see how the market area became known as "The Stones". This picture was probably taken towards the end of the last century, when the local farmers and traders brought their produce to the market by handcart, horse and cart or waggon and sold directly to the public. Produce and wares would have been carried in sacks and various baskets, which can all be seen in the picture. The few stalls visible in the distance do not seem to be well patronised.

PENKHULL STREET

This view was taken from what is now the Grosvenor Roundabout end of High Street. In the centre of the picture, the stone building was the Manchester and Liverpool District Bank. Later, the upper three stories of the building became the Town Clerk's Dept. of the Newcastle Borough Council. Tram standards, overhead cables and lines can be clearly seen and note the beautiful old motorcycle and sidecar parked outside A. Tunnicliffe's shop.

OLD HOUSES, HIGH STREET, c. 1907

This group of timber framed buildings stood in High Street, in the area now occupied by F. W. Woolworth. The opening to Friar Street can just be seen to the right of the picture. How sad it is to think that this whole block of property was demolished in the late 1950's, surely today conservation would have saved them from this fate.

Arnold's High Class Tobacconists; Waltons Dining Rooms; F. Arnold, Fruiterer; The Market Inn and Kinsey, Tailor and Hatter complete this quaint old block of shops.

IRONMARKET, c. 1914

Showing the south-west end of the Ironmarket, with its junction with High Street in the left background. The tram is waiting outside Henry Whites, Gentlemen's Outfitters, with the driver and conductor possibly standing by the tram standard. The ornate canopy outside Henry White's store, which came to the edge of the pavement, formed a good shelter in inclement weather. Read and Shaw, Ladies Outfitters, with their wares displayed can be clearly seen on the right of the picture.

CIVIC PROCESSION, IRONMARKET

The local clergy are seen leading this Civic procession in the Ironmarket. This postcard has no caption and is undated, so it is difficult to pinpoint the actual occasion. The High Constable walks ahead of the Mayor, with the Town Clerk wearing his wig, walking to his right. The people following are wearing top hats and gowns, which suggests that they could be in morning dress. The shop fronts are decorated with flags and bunting, which could have been erected for a Royal visit.

IRONMARKET, c. 1930

This view shows the central section of the Ironmarket. Two of the early omnibuses, which replaced the electric trams, can be seen, the nearest certainly being a P.M.T. vehicle but the lighter coloured one could have belonged to one of the private operators working in the area. The road surface is still formed of cobbles and the line of the old tram lines is clearly visible. To the right of the picture, the name Boyce Adams can be seen over the shop blind, a high class grocery store, loved and patronised by many local households. The black and white frontage to the George and Dragon has changed very little over the years.

JONES MOSS & CO., LATE EDWARDS, IRONMARKET, c. 1907
On the reverse of this postcard are given the details of this long established Newcastle company, Jones Moss & Co., successors to T. Edwards & Sons, est. 1797; Cabinet Makers, Upholsterers, Carpets, Removal Contractors, Decorators, Goods Warehoused, Auctioneers and Valuers. The shop and showroom shown in this picture stood in the Ironmarket on the site now occupied by Castle House. Later the Furniture Store moved to the opposite side of the Ironmarket, where it remained until some thirty years ago.

MUNICIPAL HALL AND IRONMARKET, c. 1910

The Municipal Hall stood in the Ironmarket for seventy seven years before being demolished in 1967. It was erected between 1888 and 1890 to commemorate the Golden Jubilee of Queen Victoria, and built on the site of the former Arlington House.

The Hall was a well loved landmark and a most imposing building with its magnificent clock tower.

During its life time it housed a Council Chamber, Dance Hall, School of Art, Library and Civic Restaurant.

The present Newcastle Public Library now occupies the site.

QUEEN VICTORIA'S STATUE, NELSON PLACE, 1903
This historic picture shows the unveiling of the statue of Queen Victoria in Nelson Place on 5th November, 1903. The statue was presented to the Parliamentary Borough of Newcastle-under-Lyme by Sir Alfred Seale Haslam, Kt., M.P., who was Mayor of Newcastle from 1901 to 1903. It was unveiled by H. I. H. Grand Duke Michael of Russia, who lived at Keele Hall. The statue is now to be seen in Station Walks.

QUEEN VICTORIA'S MONUMENT, NELSON PLACE, c. 1907
The monument to Queen Victoria stood in front of the old Theatre Royal, which was built in 1787-8.
This became Newcastle's first electric cinema in 1910, and was known as the Plaza.
The number of people in this scene suggest that this was a popular meeting place.

NEWCASTLE CINEMA, 1913
By this time the Newcastle Theatre had become a cinema. Later it was called the Plaza and ended its days as the Roxy, being finally demolished in 1963. Along with the rest of the town it was well decorated for the Royal visit in 1913 and an appropriate film, 'Soldiers of the King' was being shown. Note the uniformed staff including the junior with his tray of chocolates etc. lined up for this photograph. The relief medallion of Shakespeare, which was placed on the old theatre, is attributed to John Flaxman.

QUEENS PARK AND NATIONAL SCHOOL, c. 1917

The caption to this card today would read, "Queens Gardens and St. George and St. Giles' School". The Queens Gardens are now more formerly laid out, with pathways and flower beds. The National School was the first public elementary school in the Borough, built during 1825 in Bagnall Street and accommodating 600 children. The deed of foundation was dated 4th October, 1825. Many thousands of Newcastle children must have passed through this school in the past 162 years.

NELSON PLACE, 1913
A large assembly of citizens and local dignitaries waiting for the arrival of King George V and Queen Mary on their Official Visit to North Staffordshire on April 22nd, 1913
Note the decorated canopy over the dais and on the right, the statue of Queen Victoria decorated with flowers, flags and bunting.

WESLEYAN CHAPEL, BRUNSWICK STREET, c. 1905
This fine looking building known as Brunswick Street Wesleyan Chapel stood adjacent to Newcastle Swimming Baths. The Chapel was erected in 1860-61 and opened for worship in April, 1861. However, because of dwindling congregations during the 1950's, the Chapel was forced to close in 1956.
The building was acquired by Newcastle Council and was later demolished.

CONGREGATIONAL CHURCH, KING STREET, c. 1907
This Gothic style Church built in yellow and blue brick stands in King Street. It was erected in 1859 at a cost of £3,000.

EBENEZER METHODIST CHURCH AND MANSE, c. 1905

The Church was built in 1858, replacing the original Church built in 1799. It has red brick walls, with stone dressing and a slate roof. The front has an impressive entrance with stone plinth, platband and pediment. Inside there was a continuous rounded gallery.

The Church thrived for many years, but in 1977 the Church Council came to the decision that the Church maintenance costs were too high and took the decision to dispose of the building.

The congregation moved for worship to the Sunday School building in Merrial Street and continued until the new Church was constructed adjoining the school building in 1981.

The original Church was purchased by Mr. Huntbach, a local businessman, and converted into a store.

HASSELL STREET SCHOOL, 1911
Do you recognise any of these charming young girls, who attended this class at Hassell Street School, along with five year old Edith Jervis (b. 1906)? Edith is standing third from left, second row down. The School was built in 1881, and is still educating children today.

WELL STREET, c. 1912

A rare photograph of the George Inn, which stood at the corner of Barracks Road and Well Street. The placard on this free house states that A. Feazey was the licensee at this time. The George was demolished in the summer of 1987 as part of Newcastle's road improvement scheme. A plaque at the far end of the street dates the buildings from 1897. The toddler in the cowboy hat is Joe Jervis, whose father kept a shop in Garden Street.

LONDON ROAD, c. 1930
A large roundabout now exists in the foreground of this busy road junction. Small businesses occupy more of the premises today though the main structure of the buildings remain unaltered.

HOLY TRINITY CHURCH, LONDON ROAD, c. 1935

The Roman Catholic Church in London Road was constructed in 1833-4, largely through the efforts of a French priest, James Egan, who both designed and supervised its building. The north aisle was used as a school until 1865 when a separate school building was erected on the left-hand side of the Church. This school has since been replaced by the Holy Trinity Community Centre. The road is now a dual-carriageway with a large roundabout at the road junction in the background.

STUBBS WALKS, c. 1910

The Russian cannon from the Crimean War was presented to the Corporation of Newcastle by Samuel Christy, M.P. It was later to be joined by a First World War Tank. Both have now disappeared, the tank for scrap and the cannon to Newcastle museum in the Brampton. In the foreground, the smart little girl proudly poses with her doll's pram, while the newly built St. Paul's Church towers over the trees.

ST. PAUL'S CHURCH, 1905
This postcard issued by C. H. Deakin, photographer of Newcastle, shows the building of St. Paul's Church located in Victoria Road. The foundation stone was laid by Bishop Stamer on 15th June, 1905 and the Church was designed in perpendicular style by Messrs. R. Scrivener and Sons of Hanley. The building cost £8,000 with the tower and spire a further £4,500, the majority of the costs being paid for by a local benefactor, Mr. A. F. Coghill. On the photograph, three of the builders stand proudly on the unfinished spire and on the left, the uniformed boys would probably be pupils of the adjacent Newcastle High School.

ST. PAUL'S CHURCH, 1908
Another postcard issued by C. H. Deakin showing a photograph of the new Church on a mount of grained wood. The Church was consecrated by the Lord Bishop of Lichfield on 29th April, 1908 and every person, who attended the Consecration service was given one of these cards.

THE ORME GIRLS' SCHOOL, c. 1907

The Orme Girls' School was founded in 1876 and attracted pupils from a wide area, some who came by train whilst others were boarded in the town. The school was designed for one hundred girls but due to its popularity had to be enlarged in 1886. Fees were between £4 and £5 a year! The first headmistress was Miss Mary Martin, who had taught at Cheltenham Ladies College. The school became a grammar school from the first decade, and after the 1944 Education Act became a voluntary-aided school. In 1981, it became independent and merged with the Newcastle High School to be known as the Newcastle-under-Lyme School. The postcard shows the front of the school facing Victoria Road.

THE NEWCASTLE HIGH SCHOOL, 1907
The Newcastle High School for boys was built in 1876 at a cost of £12,000. It was a "first grade school" intended for those able to afford tuition fees of up to £25 a year, with an extra £50 for boarders. The school was modelled on the famous Rugby School and its first headmaster, F. E. Kitchener, had been an assistant master there. The school retained its independent status until after the 1944 Education Act when it became a voluntary-aided school under the local authority. The High School is now part of the Newcastle-under-Lyme School following the decision to become an independent school in 1981. This view is taken from Mount Pleasant.

WEST BRAMPTON, c. 1905

The Bear Hotel still stands unaltered on the corner of West Brampton and Enderley Street, just as it does in this early photograph, and is believed to have reached its centenary in 1987. An open plan corner garden site now replaces the railings and the trees on the left.

ENDERLEY MILLS

The Mills were founded in 1881 by Richard Stanway and stood on the corner of Enderley Street and Liverpool Road. The original factory included a surgery, crêche, nursery department, reading room and savings bank. Following Stanway's bankruptcy in 1884, the Mills were taken over by John Hammond and Company. Later it came under the operation of Messrs. Briggs, Jones and Gibson, with the factory producing military and service uniforms. The Mills were demolished in 1986 and the unit has been redeveloped as a Comet Warehouse.

Note the flags and shields with the top of the building dressed for a special occasion.

LIVERPOOL ROAD, c. 1909
Showing the home and part of the business premises of Sam Hughes located at 97, Liverpool Road.
Mr. Hughes was a builder and contractor and dealer in all kinds of builders materials.
Note the yard containing a very interesting selection of chimney pots.
Much of the property between Newcastle town centre and Cross Heath has now been removed.

THE BEECHES, LIVERPOOL ROAD, c. 1905

This Georgian house in Liverpool Road was later converted into a bus station. Long distance coaches called there as it was situated on the main north-south trunk road, and as the station had a large popular restaurant, known as 'The Four-in-Hand'. With the building of the M6 motorway and the Keele service station, fewer coaches made the detour to the 'Four-in-Hand restaurant'. However, in 1972, Shearings Holidays of Altrincham took on a short term lease from the P.M.T. bus company and made considerable alterations, incorporating a new self-service restaurant, two bars, steak bar and first floor restaurant to serve the seasonal trade of long distance coach travellers and holidaymakers. Sadly, the 'Four-in-Hand' proved uneconomic, Shearings withdrew their management and the building was demolished in the early 1980's leaving the P.M.T. garage remaining on the site.

ASHFIELDS SUNDAY SCHOOL

The Sunday School constructed of wood and corrugated iron was attached to the Ashfield Methodist Church, which stood on a site between Hall Street and Pratt Street, with the side of the premises overlooking Knutton Lane.
The whole area was subject to a Clearance Order by the Borough Council and in September 1975, the Church premises along with all the other properties in the area, known as "Old Ashfields" was demolished. This was at one time a thriving Church serving a closely knit community, the Sunday School Anniversary being the highlight of the year.

ST. GEORGE'S CHURCH, c. 1920

The Church was built on a piece of land called the Cherry Orchard and was opened on 18th September, 1828.

Local stone from Chapel Chorlton was used on the exterior of the building.

Since this photograph was taken, the four corner pinnacles on the tower and the gravestones in the foreground have been removed.

From the same point today, the Church is barely visible through the trees.

THE WALKS, NEWCASTLE, 1905

The Walks, or Station Walks, as it is better known, began near to Newcastle Station and continued across to West Brampton. The area shown here runs behind the houses in Sidmouth Avenue. The grassed area is somewhat enlarged now and its centre piece is Queen Victoria's statue, which originally stood in Nelson Place, until major roadworks in the early 1960's caused its removal to this site.

NEWCASTLE STATION, NORTH STAFFORDSHIRE RAILWAY, c. 1905
The station was situated just off King Street across from the Borough Arms Hotel.
The line from Stoke to Newcastle was opened in 1852 with the journey time taking five minutes.
The railway was later extended to Market Drayton in 1870.
The locomotive shown is a class 'A', 2-4-0 T, number 35 heading a down train.
On the left, the covered ramp lead from the up platform to the King Street overbridge
and the street level booking hall.

THE BRAMPTON, c. 1908

This is an unusual postcard in that it shows a wintry scene.
From the appearance of the snow it would seem that there was little traffic on the road apart from the trams.

THE BRAMPTON, c. 1910
A view up the hill towards May Bank. In the foreground, there is a double tramline enabling the cars to pass at this point. This is a truly rural scene, the fields on the left being part of Martin's farm, where the writer when a boy, remembers being sent often to fetch a pint of milk in a can.

THE BRAMPTON, c. 1920
This view is taken from where the boy is standing on the pavement on the previous page and is looking back towards Newcastle.
On the left, the house was a lodge to May Place and immediately beyond it is Sandy Lane.

HIGH STREET, MAY BANK, c. 1907
May Bank was a separate village in those days situated between the wooded fields of the Brampton and Wolstanton Marsh.

OXFORD ROAD, MAY BANK, c. 1905
This view is from the Marsh end of Oxford Road and has changed very little even today, except that the gap in the property on the left hand side has now been filled in by the building of an electricity sub-station and business premises. The corner shop on the right, unused today, has adverts for Matchless Cleaner, Venus Soap, Cadbury's Cocoa and Mackintoshes Toffee. The barber's shop indicated by a barber's pole on the right is now a private house.

MAY BANK CHAPEL AND PARADE, c. 1920
The May Bank Methodist Chapel stood in Moreton Parade until 1986, when due to falling congregations and high maintenance costs it was forced to close.
It had been a focal point for worship and Sunday School for many generations.
The church buildings have now been demolished and residential property built on the site.

THE MARSH, WOLSTANTON, c. 1905
This card shows one of the ponds, which existed on the Marsh in the early part of this century.
No doubt because of these ponds and wet areas, this it how "The Marsh" derived its name.
This scene is little changed today.
In the right background, Porthill Park cricket pavilion can be seen directly above the seat.
The photograph would have been taken from High Street looking towards Alexandra Road.

CHURCH LANE, WOLSTANTON, c. 1920

A fine view of Tram 48, advertising "Nubolic Soap", approaching High Street, Wolstanton. This scene of Wolstanton has changed little though the house on the left is surrounded by large trees, and many properties along the road have been demolished and their sites redeveloped. The white building behind the tram is the old Marshlands cinema.

S. F. BARNES (1873-1967)
Sydney Francis Barnes was born in Smethwick. He became a famous cricketer playing for Porthill Park, Staffordshire and England, and has been hailed by many as the greatest bowler in the history of cricket.
Bowling at a fast medium pace, breaking the ball both ways, coupled with swerve, subtlety of pace and perfect length proved to be a deadly combination as some of his records prove.
27 Test Matches (1901-1914),
189 wkts., average 16.43.
Staffordshire (1904-1935),
1441 wkts., average 8.15.
Porthill Park (1906-1914),
893 wkts., average 5.28.

OLD COTTAGES ON WOLSTANTON MARSH, c. 1907
This row of old cottages with one having a thatched roof stood on the Marsh.
They were situated close to the large house, which stands at the Wolstanton end of the Marsh today.
Other postcards depicting these cottages show that they stood quite close to a large pool
and an area of marshy ground.

Sparch Hollow — Wolstanton Sep. 1904
I don't know if you have
been down Sparch H. It's a
pretty walk from Newcastle.

SPARCH HOLLOW, WOLSTANTON, c. 1904
This early photograph illustrates why Sparch Hollow is so named. A leafy country lane, in a hollow, with steep grassy banks and high hedgerows.
It appears to lead directly onto the Marsh itself – just the place for a picnic or a 'spot of courting'.

HIGH STREET, WOLSTANTON, c. 1910
This splendid view taken from opposite St. Margaret's Church is much changed today. The school building on the left is now Wolstanton C. E. Junior School, and the prominent building further along has been demolished to become the Methodist Church car park. The second block of premises on the right are now replaced by a newer development of shops, flats and gardens.

HIGH STREET, WOLSTANTON, c. 1923

This photograph shows the road surface constructed of setts and the double set of tramlines, which acted as a passing loop. On the left of the picture, the wall and trees are now the site of the Wolstanton Working Men's club car park and further down, the trees in the distance are now G.E. Sparke's Garage. On the right, the overall appearance of the shops has changed very little and the nearest shop is now Wolstanton Post Office. Note how the ladies and gentlemen are happy to pose but discretely pretend to be unaware of the photographer.

HIGH STREET, WOLSTANTON, 1912

Looking down High Street in the opposite direction to page 66.
The photograph is of special historic interest as the Daily News newspaper boards outside Saunder's newsagents report the 'Titanic' disaster of 15th April, 1912, with the headline, 'Captain commits suicide as Titanic goes down'.
Note the old 'Plough' public house in the right background.

WESLEYAN CHAPEL, WOLSTANTON, c. 1908
The first Wesleyan Chapel was built on this site in 1865 and opened in 1867. In 1894, a decision was taken to demolish the existing chapel and to replace it with a new church, which was a large brick structure in the perpendicular style, with a square tower, nave and transepts.
This church was known as St. John's and flourished for many years. However, in 1979, the church was demolished and replaced with a more modern building of simpler design. Much of the stained glass from the old building has been incorporated into the new church. The former Sunday School buildings were also retained. The site of the old church is now used as a car park.

'THE LAST CAR TO WOLSTANTON', c. 1908
This design of postcard was the work of Martin Anderson, who used the pseudonym Cynicus.
His cynical wit and satirical art earned him a fortune.
This postcard of 'The Last Car' was issued with the names of many other towns,
enabling it to be sold throughout the country.

PARK AVENUE, WOLSTANTON, c. 1905
This is one of a number of residential private roads in the area, which possessed gated entrances. The gates were probably removed before the First World War. They must have been very heavy and required runners, which are clearly shown in this photograph.
At that time Park Avenue was not a through road, but now it goes through to Dimsdale Parade. Though fewer in number, trees still line the road.

THE AVENUE, PORTHILL, c. 1910
Looking towards Wolstanton from just above Porthill Church.
The large trees have gone but the decorative wall still stands.
It is difficult to understand why postcard manufacturers persisted in calling this section of the High Street, 'The Avenue'.
Did the photographer line up the children on the pavement?

ST. ANDREW'S CHURCH, PORTHILL, c. 1912

The church stands at the junction of High Street and Watlands View and has changed very little since this picture was taken. The wooden fence has now been replaced with a stone wall. A wooden cross bearing a carved figure of the Crucified Christ, a War Memorial to those killed during the 1914-18 war, now stands at the front of the building. As a result of increased population in the Wolstanton and Porthill areas, plans to build a church in Porthill commenced in 1884 and the building was eventually opened for worship in 1886. Inside the church is a large stained glass window behind the altar and flanked by two wall paintings. The five front panels to the altar also bear beautiful paintings of the Nativity. Note the two horsed dray in the foreground.

BRADWELL LANE, PORTHILL, c. 1912
This photograph is taken at the top of Porthill Bank and looking up Bradwell Lane.
On the left, the corner shop at Number Two, Watlands View was then owned by George Wood,
grocer and baker. The building now has a flat roof, with the top storey being removed
a number of years ago.

PORTHILL, c. 1905
The tram is travelling up Porthill Bank on its way to Newcastle.
It bears an advertisement for the Theatre Royal.
The large houses on the hill were mainly occupied by Burslem manufacturers.

'THE LIMES', FIRST AVENUE, PORTHILL, c. 1910
'The Limes', used to be the residence of Sydney Malkin and the photograph illustrates the lifestyle that was enjoyed by a wealthy family at this time.
The postcard was produced privately for the Malkin family for their own personal use.

PORTHILL, c. 1905
This view near the bottom of Porthill Bank is little changed today.
It must have been a heavy pull uphill for the horses and the distant cart laden with casks needed a pair of horses.
It is strange to see two wheelbarrows in this photograph.

PORTHILL, c. 1905
Looking up Porthill Bank and showing the cobbled surface on the road and the passing loop for the trams.
On the right, the side road by the railings went down to Longport station but has now disappeared beneath the A500.
Note the style of the boys' clothes.

WATLANDS VIEW, PORTHILL, c. 1930

Except for the demolition of the second block of houses on the left three years ago, little has changed over the years in Watlands View.

On the right, the photograph shows Porthill post office and at the end of the street, the tower of St. Andrew's Parish Church. Porthill roundabout is now sited at the road junction. Note that the street is surfaced and the pavements and gutter are bricked.

WATLANDS VIEW, PORTHILL, c. 1930
This busy thoroughfare was photographed looking towards Porthill roundabout
and showing the junction of Garnett Road on the right.
The scene is very similar today, but with more houses having been converted to small shops.

THE CRESCENT, WOLSTANTON, c. 1912
The Crescent along Dimsdale Parade was built in 1909 and has changed very little with the exception of additional trees and shrubs.
Note the unfortunate boy with one leg in the centre of the photograph.
His name was Jack Downing and it is thought that he lost his leg in an accident.

CORONATION PROCESSION, DIMSDALE PARADE, 1911
A splendid postcard that captures the scenes of the Coronation Day celebrations of King George V and Queen Mary, which took place on 22nd June, 1911.
The picture shows the procession marching along Dimsdale Parade opposite to the Crescent.

DIMSDALE PARADE, WOLSTANTON, c. 1910
Looking down Dimsdale Parade close to the junction with South Terrace on the left.
The trees have now been removed and must have been an unusual sight
as they were growing on the main road.
In the right foreground, the wall has been removed and is now the entrance to the
Wulstan public house.

CORONATION FESTIVAL, WOLSTANTON, 1911

The Coronation Festival of King George V was held on the Marsh adjacent to the Wulstan public house and the pathway, which has now become Dimsdale Parade. The crowd, dressed in their finery and waving flags energetically, are awaiting the raising of the flag by the gentleman at the flagpole.

The property in the background was constructed in the late nineteenth century.

On the right, a wooden Catholic Church has been replaced by the Christadelphian Hall.

SILVERDALE ROAD, c. 1910
Photographed from Wolstanton Marsh, this view looks up Silverdale Road towards the village of Wolstanton.
A garage now stands on the site of the old house on the right.

WOLSTANTON, c. 1935
A distant view of the heart of Wolstanton, taken from the highest point on Wolstanton Golf Course, adjacent to the public footpath. Hassam Parade and the housing alongside have since been built, and go right across the picture following the line of the hedge.

Dimsdale old Hall, Wolstanton.

DIMSDALE OLD HALL, WOLSTANTON, c. 1916
This view shows the rear of the Early English house, one of the few principal houses of the district, which was demolished at the turn of the century. After the Battle of Blore Heath in 1459, Queen Margaret, wife of Henry VI, stayed the night at the hall before her flight to safety. During the 16th and 17th Centuries, it was owned by the Brett family, but in 1690 was leased to John Philip Elers, who was the son of the Elector of Metz and became a Staffordshire potter with works at Bradwell Wood.
Later, the Bennett family became owners and occupiers during the 19th Century, until they built a new house close by and let the old Hall as a farm.

DIMSDALE, WOLSTANTON, c. 1912

This scene is little different today and shows the public footpath, which passes beyond the posts, which have now been replaced by concrete ones, on its way down to the A34. At this point, the lane to Wolstanton Golf Club turns sharp right. The Golf Club was formed in 1904 on the site of an old farm. On the left of the picture is the tenth tee called 'Jacob's Ladder'.

COUNTY GRAMMAR SCHOOL, WOLSTANTON, c. 1930
The Wolstanton County Grammar School was opened in 1928 to replace the Orme Boys' School in the Higherland.
The soccer posts show this to be an early photograph as rugby became the main winter game after a few years.

NEW HOUSES, MILEHOUSE LANE, c. 1920
These houses were built by the Bournville Trust at the end of World War I
principally to house returning soldiers.
They were taken over by the Newcastle Council and are quite unchanged today.

THE COTTAGES, MILEHOUSE LANE

Looking up Milehouse Lane from the junction with Liverpool Road.
The row of old cottages was probably demolished soon after this photograph was taken and was later replaced by a row of semi-detached houses, the ground floors of which serve as shops.
In the centre of the picture, the shop selling tobacco is now the Victoria Wine Company.

MILEHOUSE INN, LIVERPOOL ROAD, c. 1910
The old Milehouse Inn was situated on the corner of Milehouse Lane and Liverpool Road.
It was built in 1813 and noted for its long hours : 5.30 a.m. to 11 p.m.
This rare postcard shows many items of interest. The horse and cart bears a Knutton address and the man on the extreme left is holding a banjo. Above is a sign reading 'Pratt's spirit'.
Note the black cat behind the horse!
The new Milehouse hotel (now the Berni Tavern) was built in the 1920's on the opposite side of the road. Close to the new subway, there is a plaque with the inscription, 'Milehouse 1813'.

OLD TOLL GATE, DIMSDALE, CHESTERTON, c. 1910

This scene is looking towards the junction with London Road at Churchfields and shows the remarkable changes that have taken place along the Liverpool Road. The old Toll House stood in the area where the Comfort Friendly Inn, previously the Thomas Forshaw Hotel, is now situated.

BROADMEADOWS, CHESTERTON, c. 1910
This is now the site of a roundabout at the Hollows. On the left, the path just beyond the gate and gas lamp is now Wolstanton Road. In the centre background, can be seen 'Broadmeadow School for Infants'. It became a mixed secondary school in 1931, when the school buildings were extended. It is now 'Churchfields Nursery and Primary Schools'.

THE HOLLOWS, CHESTERTON, c. 1910
Photographed from the Hollows and showing London Road.
The gate post to the left bears the name, 'the Mount', which was then the residence of George Henry Downing.
The first building on the right is now the 'Grove House' and a little lower down the road is the junction with Beasley Avenue.

LONDON ROAD, CHESTERTON, c. 1910
Viewed looking along London Road and photographed close to the junction with Victoria Street on the left of the picture.
The plaque on the left corner shop reads, 'Victoria Buildings 1882'.
The shop appears to have been a chemists for many years.
At this time it was owned by Stathorns, but later was owned by Staniers.
On the opposite side of the road are the Co-operative Institution and Barrowdales the tailors.

LONDON ROAD, CHESTERTON, c. 1908
Photographed in the opposite direction to page 95 and viewed from a little further up the road. In the left foreground, the houses and Methodist Church were demolished some years ago. The splendid group of children were obviously fascinated by the photographer.

DRAGON SQUARE AND CHURCH STREET, CHESTERTON.

DRAGON SQUARE AND CHURCH STREET, c. 1910
Looking towards Dragon Square and photographed from the bottom of Crackley Bank. All the buildings, with the exception of Holy Trinity Church (seen centre background), have been demolished. At this time, Dragon Square was the tram terminus for the services between Newcastle and Chesterton. The tall building in the centre is the George and Dragon public house and across the road stood the Wesleyan Church.

CHESTERTON, HOLY TRINITY CHURCH

HOLY TRINITY CHURCH, CHESTERTON, c. 1905
In the mid nineteenth century, Sir Robert Peel brought an Act before Parliament, whereby provision could be made for the care and spiritual needs of the populus in Parishes. Chesterton benefited from this enactment, with the Church being built in 1853. It was built of sandstone and has changed little over the years, even the iron gates and railings have survived intact. The gravestones have been removed from the churchyard and the whole area lawned over. A feature inside this beautifully kept Church, are the four stained glass windows of the four Apostles, together with other stained glass windows behind the altar. The Church also houses one of the earliest Christian Field Crosses, dated c. 800 A.D. The cross was discovered in 1958 being used as a feed trough at Baskeyfields Farm, Red Street. It was donated to the Parish by Mr. Baskeyfield for public display.

CHESTERTON OLD HALL, c. 1904
Chesterton Old Hall was a Georgian building formerly known as Chesterton Mansion. It stood on the elevated part of Castle Street near to where the swimming baths are now situated. The 1841 census gives the occupier as Mr. Geo. Desmith and then in 1851 the occupier was Chas. Eaton, coalmaster. In 1888, the house was owned by Capt. Edwards-Heathcote of Apedale Hall and was occupied by his land agents – the first one recorded being John McDonald. It is recorded in the Transactions of the North Staffordshire Field Club that in 1925, Mr. Trickett allowed Mr. T. Pape to excavate in the garden, though the hoped for traces of Roman occupation did not materialise.

CHESTERTON POST OFFICE, c. 1914
The Post Office is situated in Victoria Street by the junction with King Street. In the days of trans-Atlantic shipping, it served as a booking office for the Canadian Pacific Shipping Company and the Cunard Line. Among the newspaper headlines on the boards, are details of the budget in the Daily Dispatch and the Chester Cup in the Daily Sketch. The Post Office has now moved from these premises which are still used as a small shop.

APEDALE HALL, c. 1925
Apedale Hall was built in 1826 by Richard Edensor Heathcote of Longton Hall, who was associated with the industry of Apedale.
The lawns in front of the hall were often used for festive occasions by the local people.
After the Heathcotes left the Hall in 1928, it was occupied for a time by the manager of the Midland Coal, Coke and Iron Company.
Later, no buyer could be found for the Hall and in 1934 it was demolished.

LOVER'S WALK, CHESTERTON, c. 1910
This delightful and romantic scene at Watermills Wood, Apedale will no doubt bring back many happy memories!

APEDALE FURNACES, CHESTERTON, c. 1912

The first furnace at Apedale was put into blast by Abraham Parker in 1789, under lease from Sir Nigel Gresley. From 1820 until 1838, the ironworks were leased by Thomas Firmstone from the executors of Gresley, who had died in 1808. The ironworks were then taken over by Robert Edensor Heathcote, who by this time owned the Apedale estate. Between 1860 and 1888, Francis Stanier held the lease during which time he merged the Apedale and Silverdale works and with Robert Heath built Knutton Forge. By the time he retired he had become a millionaire. In 1890, the Midland Coal, Coke and Iron Company was formed out of the various industrial interests of the estate, taking over the running of the ironworks and collieries. The iron they produced was sold to South Staffordshire merchants and forgers. In 1930, the Midland Company went bankrupt, resulting in three thousand men out of work. The whole estate was demolished and sold for scrap by Thomas W. Ward in the early 1930's.

COAL PICKERS, CHESTERTON

This card is a 'gem' for any post card collector, depicting a unique event of local social history, coal pickers in Chesterton. The card is not dated and it could have been taken during one of the coal strikes, perhaps 1912 or 1921. Times were hard and coal picking was well organised, note the picks, shovels, sieves and the old wooden wheelbarrow.

The dress is typical of the 1920's with all the men wearing caps and also note how one woman and some children are involved.

WAR MEMORIAL GALA, CHESTERTON

A charming group of ladies and children all in their Sunday best outside the refreshment tent at the Chesterton War Memorial Gala held on the 21st July, 1919.
The ladies' hats based on a simple style, shows an enormous variety of decorative trimmings, indicative of the costume of those times.

RED STREET, CHESTERTON, c. 1912

This postcard shows many of the old properties that once stood in this part of Red Street. The Crown Hotel in the foreground and a few of the terraced houses towards the end of the street are all that remain today. Many local residents will no doubt remember the two small corner shops close to the horse and cart on the right of the picture.

RED STREET, CHESTERTON, c. 1912

A superb postcard showing one of Richard Howle's horse-drawn furniture removal vans, standing outside the Crown Hotel at the corner of Deans Lane, Red Street. Richard Howle, who kept the Wheatsheaf public house in Red Street, was also well known in the area for his steam driven traction engines. The white building in the background, later became the Anchor public house, but is now a private residence.

HIGH STREET, KNUTTON, c. 1925
This view of the High Street was photographed from the corner of Nash Street and is looking towards Blackbank Road.
This part of the High Street looks much the same today except for the absence of the trees and the addition of a small shop built at the corner of Nash Street.

ARTHUR STREET, KNUTTON, c. 1914
An historically important photograph of a typical row of miner's houses in Knutton.
Note the wide entrance that gave access to the back of the houses,
the gravel road surface and wooden palings.
Few photographic records can exist as the houses were demolished to be replaced
by Council housing, though the street and its original name have been kept.

SILVERDALE FURNACES

The furnaces at Silverdale stood in the area now adjacent to Furnace Pool, Scot Hay Road. These furnaces were operated by Francis Stanier, who also controlled most of the coalmines in the area. Stanier was thus able to supply the furnaces with coal mined locally. However, because of fierce competition in the steel industry, Stanier decided not to renew his leases on the Silverdale furnaces and mines, which resulted in the furnaces being closed in the 1880's.

CHURCH AND NEWCASTLE STREET, SILVERDALE, c. 1910
This busy street scene is looking in the direction of Newcastle Road.
Much of the street looks the same today, although a number of the shops and houses on the right were demolished some years ago and have since been replaced by a small park and recreational area.

CHURCH STREET, SILVERDALE, c. 1910
Photographed at the top of Church Street and illustrating how this part of the village looked when Silverdale was linked to Newcastle by electric tram (1901-1928).
On the left, the cottages have now been demolished and replaced with a row of modern houses.
The building on the extreme right is now the Silverdale Conservative Club.

SNEYD TERRACE, SILVERDALE, c. 1904

This scene is very similar today and shows a typical row of terraced houses, for residents, who were a little "better off". The houses have bay windows and small forecourts with iron railings. The tram lines and wires are clearly visible but the only form of transport on the scene is a horse and cart at the far end of the terrace.

ST. LUKE'S CHURCH, SILVERDALE, c. 1925

St. Luke's Church was opened in 1853 and is constructed of sandstone quarried in Hollywood, the stone being donated by the Sneyd family of Keele Hall. The internal pillars are of Hollington stone. A feature inside of the Church are the beautiful stained glass windows, there is also a carved wood screen erected in memory to those who gave their lives in the First World War. A large plaque in the Church is dedicated to Francis Stanier Esq., who died at Madeley Manor in 1856. The plaque was erected by his agent and workers in recognition of the services he rendered to the community through industrial and social improvements. The grounds of the Church are now lawned, the headstones having been moved to the rear of the Church. Alas the tower of the Church is now in a dangerous condition due to mining subsidence and the whole building is threatened with closure.

ST. LUKE'S, SILVERDALE

The Clergy and Parishioners proudly displaying their new bells, which were installed in 1907. Prior to this date, they were taken around the village by horse and cart. A plaque to commemorate this event, can be found in the Church and reads: "To the Glory of God, this peel of bells, erected by voluntary subscriptions of Parishioners and the Masonic and other friends of the Vicar at a cost of £500, was dedicated by Ven. J. H. Crump M.A., Archdeacon of Stoke-on-Trent on St. Luke's Eve Oct. 17th A.D. 1907.

W. C. V. Vaughan B.A., Vicar. J. Warner & Sons, Bell Founders.

C. M. N. Sharpe, Ass't. Curate. A. P. Street & J. France, Church Wardens."

Sadly, because of the dangerous condition of the church tower, the bells can no longer be rung.

SILVERDALE STATION, NORTH STAFFORDSHIRE RAILWAY, c. 1918
Silverdale was one of the stations situated on the Stoke to Market Drayton line. Passenger services from Stoke to Silverdale commenced in 1863, with the line being extended to Market Drayton by 1870. The service lasted for over a century, with the last passenger train between Silverdale and Stoke running in March, 1964. A single line from Apedale to Madeley Chord, which transports coal trains from Holditch and Silverdale collieries, is one of the few reminders of this once prosperous railway. This photograph of the station is looking in an easterly direction and showing the spire of St. Luke's Church in the background. The building on the extreme right was the station master's house.

THE BRIGHTON, SILVERDALE, c. 1920
The Brighton was the name given to a row of very old stone cottages that were situated close to St. Luke's Church and the railway line. They were sadly demolished in c. 1960 and have since been replaced by a row of bungalows for retired people.

WEST END TERRACE, SILVERDALE, c. 1910
This view is taken in High Street, Silverdale, at its junction with Kinsey Street.
The street name can be seen on the gable of the terrace on the right of the picture.
The trees in the centre have mostly disappeared and the area is now occupied by houses.
Note the tram lines and standards and the dress of the two children walking down High Street.

RED HEATH ROAD, SILVERDALE, c. 1908
This tranquil scene in Red Heath Road (now Pepper Street) is looking in the direction towards the junction with Silverdale High Street.
These old cottages still remain today and stand across from the corner of Underwood Road.

VIEW FROM RED HEATH, SILVERDALE, c. 1920
The large residence to the right of the picture, was the old St. Lukes vicarage which fronted onto Pepper Street. The vicarage was demolished some years ago and a modern vicarage constructed on the site. The building in the centre of the picture still stands today and is known as Vicarage Cottage, which also faces onto Pepper Street. Immediately above this cottage, where the goalposts to the football pitch can be seen, is now the entrance to Underwood Road. The football pitch was used by the St. Luke's Church team.

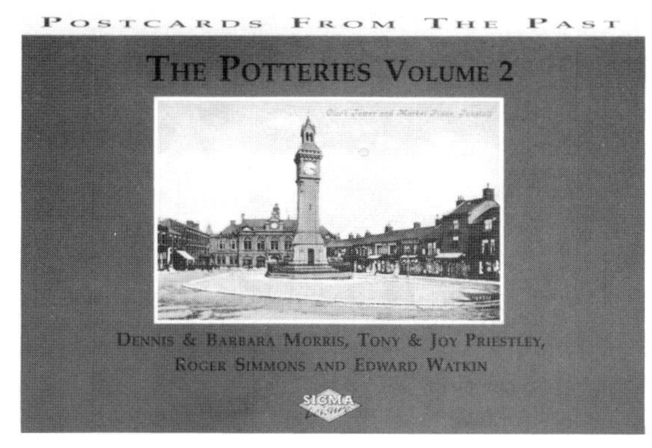

POSTCARDS FROM THE PAST: THE POTTERIES, Volumes I and II

Dennis Morris, Tony and Joy Priestley, Roger Simmons and Edward Watkin

Volume I covers the renowned "six towns" – Tunstall, Burslem, Hanley, Stoke, Fenton and Longton. Volume II includes many views of the villages within the city boundaries, together with many views of the pottery industry and potters at work.

£6.95 per volume

POSTCARDS FROM THE PAST: KIDSGROVE, TALKE & MOW COP

Roger Simmons

The collieries of the area form the backdrop to this collection, with many of the original streets once occupied by miners' families being replaced by modern developments. There are views of Mow Cop, the birthplace of primitive Methodism, and other local heritage sites.

£6.95

THE POTTERIES: the way they were

Donald Morris

This unique, large format, collection of photographs captures the essence of the architecture, atmosphere and craftsmanship of the pottery industry which once characterised Stoke-on-Trent. Taken just before the demolition of the bottle-ovens and the demise of the saggar maker's craft, the eye of Donald Morris' camera falls on potters at their workplace, canals, domestic buildings, gas lamps and many other features of Stoke-on-Trent from the 1950s to the 1970s. Born in the town in 1925, Donald Morris' grandfather and great-grandfather were both master potters. His sharp, stylish photographs are a nostalgic record of Stoke-on-Trent's past, and the result of a highly individual artistic vision.

£9.95

Sigma Leisure books are available from all booksellers. In case of difficulty, or for a free catalogue, please contact:
SIGMA LEISURE, 1 SOUTH OAK LANE, WILMSLOW, CHESHIRE SK9 6AR. *Phone: 01625-531035; Fax: 01625-536800.*
E-mail: sigma.press@zetnet.co.uk . Web site: http//www.sigmapress.co.uk
Credit card orders welcome. Please add £2 p&p to all orders.